Akhenaten

The Heretic Pharaoh

Authored by Brien Foerster
Front cover by Marcia K. Moore

Dedication

This book is about an ancient man of nobility who grew up in a system that he found unjust; not only for himself and his family, but his nation. I dedicate it to all those that stand up for what they believe, no matter what the cost. On a more personal level, my deepest thanks to author Stephen Mehler, who has been passionate about Akhenaten and ancient Egypt in general for most of his life. To my mother Ann, who always supported my pursuits and choices, and to my beloved Irene, who walks with me always.

Table Of Contents

1. Introduction

2. The Early Years As Amenhotep IV

3. Changing Of His Name To Akhenaten

4. The Aten Belief System

5. The Artistic Depictions

6. The Children Of Akhenaten

7. International Relations

8. Death And Royal Succession And The Aten Belief System

9. Akhetaten

10. Conclusions

1. Introduction

Akhenaten, who was known before the fifth year of his reign as Amenhotep IV was a pharaoh of the Eighteenth dynasty of Egypt who ruled for 17 years and died perhaps in 1336 or 1334 BC. He is especially noted for abandoning the then traditional Egyptian polytheism religious system and introducing worship centered on the Aten, which is sometimes described as monotheistic or henotheistic. An early inscription likens the Aten to the sun as compared to stars, and later official language avoids calling the Aten a god, and thereby giving the solar deity a status above mere gods.

Although he tried to bring about a departure from the traditional religion of the time, in the end it would not be accepted. After his death, traditional polytheistic religious practice was gradually restored, and when some dozen years later rulers without clear rights of succession from the Eighteenth Dynasty founded a new dynasty, they discredited Akhenaten and his immediate successors, referring to Akhenaten himself as "the enemy" or "that criminal" in archival records.

He was all but lost from history until the discovery, in the 19th century, of Amarna, the site of Akhetaten, the city he built for the Aten. Early excavations at Amarna by archaeologist William Flinders Petrie sparked interest in the enigmatic pharaoh, whose tomb was unearthed in 1907 in a dig led by Edward R. Ayrton. Interest in

Akhenaten then increased with the discovery in the Valley of the Kings, at Luxor, of the tomb of King Tutankhamun, who has been suggested to be Akhenaten's son according to DNA testing done in 2010.

Howard Carter, on the left, discoverer of Tutankhamun's tomb

A mummy found in KV55 in 1907 has been identified as that of Akhenaten. This man and Tutankhamun are related without question, but the identification of the KV55 mummy as Akhenaten has been questioned by many.

Modern interest in Akhenaten and his queen, Nefertiti, comes partly from his connection with Tutankhamun, partly from the unique style and high quality of the pictorial arts he patronized, and partly from ongoing interest in the religion he attempted to establish, or some would suggest re-establish.

Artwork from the time of Akhenaten

2. The Early Years As Amenhotep IV

The future Akhenaten was a younger son of Amenhotep III and Chief Queen Tiye. Their eldest son, Thutmose, was recognized as the heir of Amenhotep III but he died relatively young and the next in line for the throne was Amenhotep IV.

There is much controversy around whether Amenhotep IV succeeded to the throne on the death of his father, Amenhotep III, or whether there was a coregency (lasting as long as 12 years according to some Egyptologists). Current literature by Eric Cline, Nicholas Reeves, Peter Dorman and other scholars comes out strongly against the establishment of a long coregency between the two rulers and in favour of either no coregency or a brief one lasting one to two years at the most. Other literature by Donald Redford, William Murnane, Alan Gardiner and more recently by Lawrence Berman in 1998 contests the view of any coregency whatsoever between Akhenaten and his father.

In February 2014, Egyptian Ministry for Antiquities announced what it called conclusive evidence that Akhenaten shared power with his father for at least 8 years. The evidence came from the inscriptions found in the Luxor tomb of Vizier Amenhotep-Huy and a team of Spanish archeologists have been working at this tomb since that time.

Amenhotep IV was crowned in Thebes and there he started a building program. He decorated the southern entrance to the precincts of the temple of Amun-Re with scenes of himself worshipping Re-Harakhti. He soon decreed the construction of a temple dedicated to the Aten at the Eastern Karnak.

This Temple of Amenhotep IV was called the *Gempaaten* ("The Aten is found in the estate of the Aten"). The Gempaaten consisted of a series of buildings, including a palace and a structure called the *Hwt Benben* which was dedicated to Queen Nefertiti. Other Aten temples constructed at Karnak during this time include the Rud-menu and the Teni-menu which may have been constructed near the Ninth Pylon. During this time he did not repress the worship of Amun, and the High Priest of Amun was still active in the fourth year of his reign. The pharaoh appears represented as Amenhotep IV in the tombs of some of the nobles in Thebes: Kheruef (TT192),

Ramose (TT55)   and   the   tomb of Parennefer (TT188).

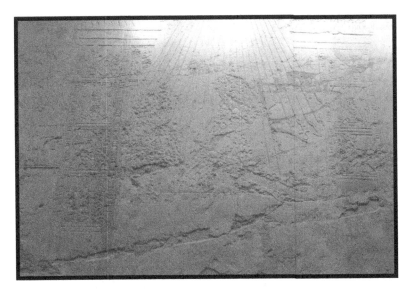

Tomb of Ramose

In the tomb of Ramose, Amenhotep IV appears on the west wall in the traditional style, seated on a throne with Ramose appearing before the ruler. On the other side of the doorway Amenhotep IV and Nefertiti are shown in the window of appearance with the Aten depicted as the sun disc. In the

Theban tomb of Parennefer, Amenhotep IV and Nefertiti are seated on a throne with the sun disk depicted over the king and queen.

One of the last known documents referring to Amenhotep IV are two copies of a letter from the Steward Of Memphis Apy (or Ipy) to the Pharaoh. The documents were found in Gurob and are dated to reign year 5, 3rd month of the Growing Season, day 19.

3. Changing Of His Name To Akhenaten

On day 13, Month 8, in the fifth year of his reign, Akhenaten arrived at the site of the new city Akhetaten (now known as Amarna). A month before that Amenhotep IV had officially changed his name to Akhenaten and most of his 5 titles in the same year. The only name he kept was his praenomen or throne name.

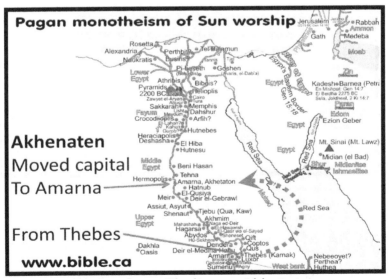

Moving from Thebes to Akhetaten

4. The Aten Belief System

Some recent debate has focused on the extent to which Akhenaten forced his religious reforms on his people. Certainly, as time drew on, he revised the names of the Aten, and other religious language to increasingly exclude references to other gods; at some point, also, he embarked on the wide-scale erasure of traditional gods' names, especially those of Amun.

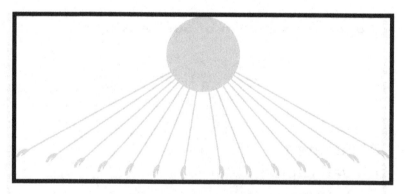

Symbol of the Aten

Some of his court changed their names to remove them from the patronage of other gods and place them under that of Aten (or Ra, with whom Akhenaten equated the Aten). Yet, even at Amarna itself, some courtiers kept such names as Ahmose ("child of the moon god", the owner of tomb 3), and the sculptor's workshop where the famous Nefertiti bust, and other works of royal portraiture, were found, is associated with an artist known to have been called Thutmose ("child of Thoth"). An overwhelmingly large number of faience amulets at Amarna also show that talismans of the household and childbirth gods Bes and Taweret, the eye of Horus, and amulets of other traditional deities, were openly worn by its citizens. Indeed, a cache of royal jewelry found buried near the Amarna royal tombs (now in the National Museum of

Scotland) includes a finger ring referring to Mut, the wife of Amun. Such evidence suggests that though Akhenaten shifted funding away from traditional temples, his policies were fairly tolerant until some point, perhaps a particular event as yet unknown, toward the end of the reign.

Cartouche of Mut

Following Akhenaten's death, change was gradual at first. Within a decade a comprehensive political, religious and artistic reformation began promoting a return of Egyptian life to the norms it had followed during his father's reign. Much of the art and building infrastructure created during Akhenaten's reign was defaced or destroyed in the period following his death, particularly during the reigns of Horemheb and the early Nineteenth Dynasty kings. Stone building blocks from Akhenaten's construction projects were later used as foundation stones for subsequent rulers' temples and tombs.

Akhetaten as seen today

5. The Artistic Depictions

Styles of art that flourished during this short period are markedly different from other Egyptian art. In some cases, representations are more naturalistic, especially in depictions of animals and plants, of commoners, and in a sense of action and movement for both non royal and royal people.

Natural style of the Amarna period

However, depictions of members of the court, especially members of the royal family, are extremely stylized, with elongated heads, protruding stomachs, heavy hips, thin arms and legs, and exaggerated facial features. Significantly, and for the only time in the history of Egyptian royal art, Akhenaten's family are shown taking part in decidedly naturalistic activities, showing affection for each other, and being caught in mid-action (in traditional art, a pharaoh's divine nature was expressed by repose, even immobility).

The depictions of action may correspond to the emphasis on the active, creative nurturing of the Aten emphasized in the "Great Hymn to the Aten" and elsewhere.

Two of the daughters of Akhenaten and Nefertiti

Questions also remain whether the beauty of Nefertiti is portraiture or idealism. Nefertiti also appears, both beside the king and alone (or with her daughters), in actions usually reserved for a Pharaoh, suggesting that she enjoyed unusual status for a queen. Early artistic representations of her tend to be indistinguishable from her husband's except by her regalia, but soon after the move to the new capital, Nefertiti begins to be depicted with features specific to her.

Classic portrait of the royal family

Why Akhenaten had himself represented in the bizarre, strikingly androgynous way he did, remains a vigorously debated question. Religious reasons have been suggested, such as to emulate the creative nature of the

Aten, who is called in Amarna tomb texts, "mother and father" of all that is. Or, it has been suggested, Akhenaten's (and his family's) portraiture exaggerates his distinctive physical traits. Until Akhenaten's mummy is positively identified, such theories remain speculative. Some scholars do identify Mummy 61074, found in KV55, an unfinished tomb in the Valley of the Kings, as Akhenaten's. If so, or if the KV 55 mummy is that of his close relative, Smenkhkare, its measurements tend to support the theory that Akhenaten's depictions exaggerate his actual appearance. Though the "mummy" consists only of disarticulated bones, the skull is long and has a prominent chin, and the Limbs are light and long. In 2007, Zahi

Statue of Akhenaten in the Cairo Museum

Hawass and a team of researchers made CT scan images of Mummy 61074. They have concluded that the elongated skull, cheek bones, cleft palate, and impacted wisdom tooth suggest that the mummy is the father of Tutankhamun, and thus is Akhenaten. However, simple visual comparisons such as this are hardly strong scientific evidence.

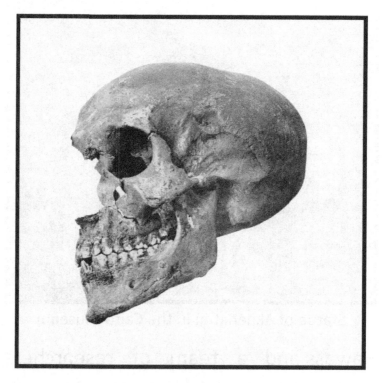

Proposed skull of Akhenaten

6. The Children Of Akhenaten

As Amenhotep IV, Akhenaten was married to Nefertiti at the very beginning of his reign, and six daughters were identified from inscriptions as being theirs. Recent DNA analysis has revealed that with one of his biological sisters, the "Younger Lady" mummy, Akhenaten may have fathered Tutankhaten (later Tutankhamen).

The parentage of Smenkhkare, his successor, is unknown, and Akhenaten and an unknown wife have been proposed to be his parents by some researchers.

A secondary wife of Akhenaten named Kiya is known from inscriptions. Some have theorized that she gained her importance as the mother of

Tutankhamen, Smenkhkare, or both, but as the body of Akhenaten has not been identified or even necessarily found, this is speculation based on almost no data.

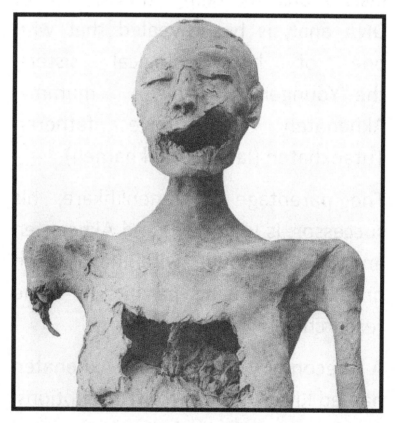

Mummy of the "Younger Lady"

This is a list of Akhenaten's children (known and theoretical) with suggested years of birth:

Smenkhkare – year 35 or 36 of Amenhotep III's reign.

Meritaten – year 1.

Meketaten – year 3, possibly earlier.

Ankhesenpaaten, later Queen of Tutankhamun – year 4.

Neferneferuaten Tasherit – year 8.

Neferneferure – year 9.

Setepenre – year 9.

Tutankhaten – year 8 or 9 – renamed Tutankhamun later.

His known consorts were:

- Nefertiti, his Great Royal Wife.
- Kiya, a lesser Royal Wife.

- A daughter of Šatiya, ruler of Enišasi

- A daughter of Burna-Buriash, King of Babylon

It has been proposed that Akhenaten may have taken some of his daughters as sexual consorts, to attempt to father a male heir by them, but this is very debatable. It does seem certain that like his father, Amenhotep III, Akhenaten named at least one daughter as Great Royal Wife. But this does not necessarily indicate she was his sexual consort as the position was also an important ceremonial position.

Meritaten is recorded as Great Royal Wife to Smenkhkare in the tomb of Meryre II in Akhet-Aten. She is also listed alongside King Akhenaten and King Neferneferuaten as Great Royal

Wife on a box from the tomb of Tutankhamen. Letters written to Akhenaten from foreign rulers make reference to Meritaten as 'mistress of the house'.

Meketaten, Akhenaten's second daughter's death in childbirth is recorded in the royal tombs of Amarna about the year 13 or 14. Since no husband is known for her, the assumption has been that Akhenaten was the father. The inscription giving the filiation of the child are damaged to prevent resolving the issue.

Various monuments originally for Kiya, were reinscribed for Akhenaten's daughters Meritaten and Ankhesenpaaten, the revised inscriptions list a Meritaten-Tasherit ("junior") and an Ankhesenpaaten-

Tasherit. Some view this to indicate that Akhenaten fathered his own grandchildren. Others hold that since these grandchildren are not attested to elsewhere, that they are fictions invented to fill in the space originally filled by Kiya's child.

Two other lovers have been suggested, but are not widely accepted; Smenkhkare, Akhenaten's successor and/or co-ruler for the last years of his reign. Rather than a lover, however, Smenkhkare is likely to have been a half-brother or a son to Akhenaten. Some have even suggested that Smenkhkare was actually an alias of Nefertiti or Kiya, and therefore one of Akhenaten's wives.

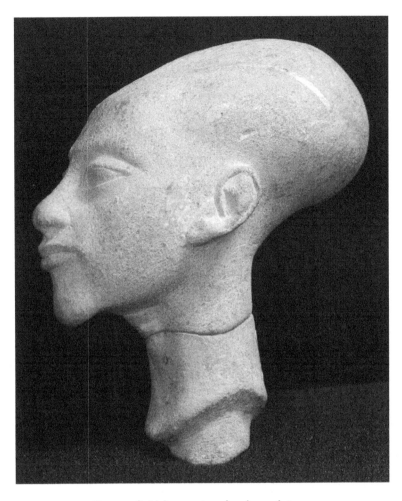

One of Akhenaten's daughters

And regarding Tiye, Akhenaten's mother. Twelve years after the death of Amenhotep III, she is still mentioned in inscriptions as Queen and beloved of the King, but kings' mothers often were. The few supporters of this theory (notably Immanuel Velikovsky) consider Akhenaten to be the historical model of legendary King Oedipus of Thebes, Greece and Tiye the model for his mother/wife Jocasta.

Bust of Queen Tiye

7. International Relations

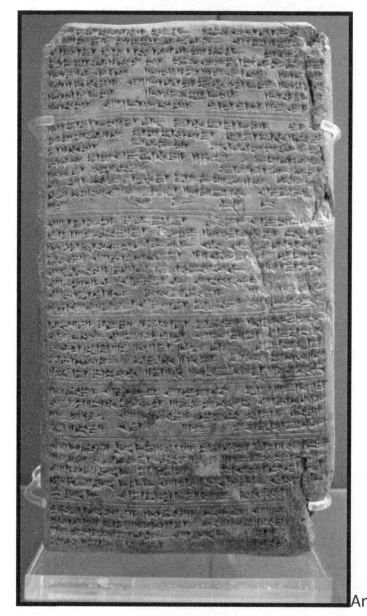

Amarna letter EA-19

The Amarna Letters, a cache of diplomatic correspondence discovered in modern times at el-Amarna (the modern designation of the site of Akhetaten) have provided important evidence about Akhenaten's reign and foreign policy. This correspondence comprises a priceless collection of incoming messages on clay tablets, sent to Akhetaten from various subject rulers through Egyptian military outposts, and from the foreign rulers (recognized as "Great Kings") of the kingdoms of Mitanni, Babylon, Assyria and Hatti. The governors and kings of Egypt's subject domains also wrote frequently to plead for gold from the Pharaoh, and also complained that he had snubbed and cheated them.

Early in his reign, Akhenaten fell out with the king of Mitanni, named Tushratta, who had courted favour with his father against the Hittites. Nefertiti is said to have come from the Mitanni bloodline. Tushratta complains in numerous letters that Akhenaten had sent him gold-plated statues rather than statues made of solid gold; the statues formed part of the bride-price which Tushratta received for letting his daughter Tadukhepa marry first Amenhotep III and then Akhenaten. Amarna letter EA 27 preserves a complaint by Tushratta to Akhenaten about the situation:

"I...asked your father, Mimmureya, for statues of solid cast gold, one of myself and a second statue, a statue of Tadu-Heba (Tadukhepa), my daughter, and your father said, 'Don't talk of giving statues just of solid cast gold. I will give you ones made also of lapis lazuli. I will give you, too, along with the statues, much additional gold and (other) goods beyond measure.'

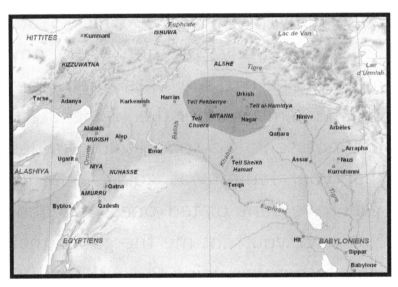

The Mitanni Kingdom

Every one of my messengers that were staying in Egypt saw the gold for the statues with their own eyes. Your father himself recast the statues in the presence of my messengers, and he made them entirely of pure gold....He showed much additional gold, which was beyond measure and which he was sending to me. He said to my messengers, 'See with your own eyes, here the statues, there much gold and goods beyond measure, which I am sending to my brother.' And my messengers did see with their own eyes! But my brother (i.e.: Akhenaten) has not sent the solid (gold) statues that your father was going to send. You have sent plated ones of wood. Nor have you sent me the goods that your father was going to send me, but you have reduced (them) greatly. Yet there is nothing I know of in which I have failed my brother. Any day that I hear the greetings of my brother, that day I make a festive occasion... May my brother send me much gold. With many goods may my brother honor me. In my brother's country gold is as plentiful as dust. May my brother cause me no distress. May he send me much gold in order that my brother may honor me."

While Akhenaten was certainly not a close friend of Tushratta, he was evidently concerned at the expanding power of the Hittite Empire under its powerful ruler Suppiluliuma I. A successful Hittite attack on Mitanni and its ruler Tushratta would have disrupted the entire international balance of power in the Ancient Middle East at a time when Egypt had made peace with Mitanni. This would cause some of Egypt's vassals to switch their allegiances to the Hittites, as time would prove. A group of Egypt's allies who attempted to rebel against the Hittites were captured, and wrote letters begging Akhenaten for troops, but he did not respond to most of their pleas. Evidence suggests that the troubles on the northern frontier led to difficulties in Canaan, particularly in a struggle for power between Labaya of Shechem and Abdi-Heba of Jerusalem, which required the Pharaoh to intervene in the area by dispatching Medjay troops northwards. Akhenaten pointedly refused to save his vassal Rib-Hadda of Byblos; whose kingdom was being besieged by the expanding state of Amurru under Abdi-Ashirta and later Aziru, son of Abdi-Ashirta; despite Rib-Hadda's numerous pleas for help from the pharaoh.

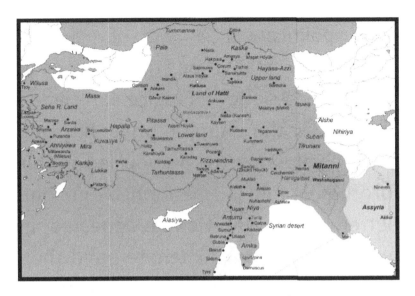

Hittite Empire circa 1300 B.C.

Rib-Hadda wrote a total of 60 letters to Akhenaten pleading for aid from the Pharaoh. Akhenaten wearied of Rib-Hadda's constant correspondences and once told him: *"You are the one that writes to me more than all the (other) mayors"* or Egyptian vassals in EA 124. What Rib-Hadda did not comprehend was that the Egyptian king would not organize and dispatch an entire army north just to preserve the political *status quo* of several minor city states on the fringes of Egypt's Asiatic Empire. Rib-Hadda would pay the ultimate price; his exile from Byblos due to a coup led by his brother Ilirabih is mentioned in one letter. When Rib-Hadda appealed in vain for aid from Akhenaten and then turned to Aziru, his sworn enemy, to place him back on the throne of his city, Aziru promptly had him dispatched to the king of Sidon, where Rib-Hadda was almost certainly executed.

William L. Moran notes that the Amarna corpus of 380 plus letters counters the conventional view that Akhenaten neglected Egypt's foreign territories in favour of his internal reforms. Several letters from Egyptian vassals notify the Pharaoh that they have followed his instructions:

'To the king, my lord, my god, my Sun, the Sun from the sky: Message of Yapahu, the ruler of Gazru, your servant, the dirt at your feet. I indeed prostrate myself at the feet of the king, my lord, my god, my Sun...7 times and 7 times, on the stomach and on the back. I am indeed guarding the place of the king, my lord, the Sun of the sky, where I am, and all the things the king, my lord, has written me, I am indeed carrying out--everything! Who am I, a dog, and what is my house... and what is anything I have, that the orders of the king, my lord, the Sun from the sky, should not obey constantly?' *(EA 378)*

When the loyal but unfortunate Rib-Hadda was killed at the instigation of

Aziru, Akhenaten sent an angry letter to Aziru containing a barely veiled accusation of outright treachery on the latter's part. Akhenaten wrote:

'Say to Aziru, ruler of Amurru: Thus the king, your lord (i.e.: Akhenaten), saying: The ruler of Gubla (i.e.: Byblos), whose brother had cast him away at the gate, said to you, "Take me and get me into the city. There is much silver, and I will give it to you. Indeed there is an abundance of everything, but not with me [here]." Thus did the ruler (Rib-Hadda) speak to you. Did you not write to the king, my lord saying, "I am your servant like all the previous mayors (i.e.: vassals) in his city"? Yet you acted delinquently by taking the mayor whose brother had cast him away at the gate, from his city.'

'He (Rib-Hadda) was residing in Sidon and, following your own judgment, you gave him to (some) mayors. Were you ignorant of the treacherousness of the men? If you really are the king's servant, why did you not denounce him before the king, your lord, saying, "This mayor has written to me saying, 'Take me to yourself and get me into my city'"? And if you did act loyally, still all the things you wrote were not true. In fact, the king has reflected on them as follows, "Everything you have said is not friendly."

Now the king has heard as follows, 'You are at peace with the ruler of Qidsa. (Kadesh) The two of you take food and strong drink together. And it is true. Why do you act so? Why are you at peace with a ruler whom the king is fighting? And even if you did act loyally, you considered your own judgment, and his judgment did not count. You have paid no attention to the things that you did earlier. What happened to you among them that you are not on the side of the king, your lord?

Sidon

Consider the people that are training you for their own advantage. They want to throw you into the fire....If for any reason whatsoever you prefer to do evil, and if you plot evil, treacherous things, then you, together with your entire family, shall die by the axe of the king. So perform your service for the king, your lord, and you will live. You yourself know that the king does not fail when he rages against all of Canaan. And when you wrote saying, "May the king, my Lord, give me leave this year, and then I will go next year to the king, my Lord. (i.e.: to Egypt) If this is impossible, I will send my son in my place" - the king, your Lord, let you off this year in accordance with what you said. Come yourself, or send your son [now], and you will see the king at whose sight all lands live.' (EA 162)

This letter shows that Akhenaten paid close attention to the affairs of his vassals in Canaan and Syria. He commanded Aziru to come to Egypt and proceeded to detain him there for at least one year. In the end, Akhenaten was forced to release Aziru back to his homeland when the Hittites advanced southwards into Amki, thereby threatening Egypt's series of Asiatic vassal states, including Amurru. Sometime after his return to Amurru, Aziru defected to the Hittite side with his kingdom.

While it is known from an Amarna letter by Rib-Hadda that the Hittites "seized all the countries that were vassals of the king of Mitanni" (EA 75) Akhenaten managed to preserve Egypt's control over the core of her

Near Eastern Empire (which consisted of present-day Israel as well as the Phoenician coast) while avoiding conflict with the increasingly powerful Hittite Empire of Suppiluliuma I. Only the Egyptian border province of Amurru in Syria around the Orontes River was permanently lost to the Hittites when its ruler Aziru defected to them. Finally, contrary to the conventional view of a ruler who neglected Egypt's international relations, Akhenaten is known to have initiated at least one campaign into Nubia in his reigning year 12, where his campaign is mentioned in Amada stela CG 41806 and on a separate companion stela at Buhen.

8. Death And Royal Succession And The Aten Belief System

Limestone stela in the Cairo Museum

The last dated appearance of Akhenaten and the Amarna family is in the tomb of Meryra II, and dates from second month, year 12 of his reign. After this the historical record is unclear, and only with the succession of Tutankhamun is somewhat clarified.

However, recently, in December 2012, it was announced that a Year 16 III Akhet day 15 inscription dated explicitly to Akhenaten's reign which mentions, in the same breath, the presence of a living Queen Nefertiti, has now been found in a limestone quarry at Deir el-Bersha just north of Amarna. The text refers to a building project in Amarna. It establishes that Akhenaten and Nefertiti were still a royal couple just a year prior to Akhenaten's death.

Akhenaten planned to relocate Egyptian burials on the East side of the Nile (sunrise) rather than on the West side (sunset), in the Royal Wadi in Akhetaten. His proposed body was removed after the court returned to Thebes, and again recent genetic tests have supposedly confirmed that

Uncompleted bust of Nefertiti

the body found buried in tomb KV55 was the father of Tutankhamun, and is therefore "most probably" Akhenaten, although this is disputed to this day. The tomb contained numerous Amarna era objects including a royal funerary mask which had been deliberately destroyed. His sarcophagus was destroyed but has since been reconstructed and now sits outside in the Cairo Museum.

Proposed sarcophagus of Akhenaten

It is believed by some, notably author Stephen Mehler that such was the hatred of Akhenaten by the Amen priesthood whom he deposed, that his body, and perhaps those of Nefertiti and their children (except Tutankhamun if he was his son) were savagely cut into pieces. By doing so, they could never move forward into the next, or any other life.

Similarly, although it is accepted that Akhenaten himself died in Year 17 of his reign, the question of whether Smenkhkare became co-regent perhaps two or three years earlier or enjoyed a brief independent reign is unclear. If Smenkhkare outlived Akhenaten, and became sole Pharaoh, he likely ruled Egypt for less than a year. The next successor was Neferneferuaten, a female Pharaoh who reigned in Egypt for two years and one month. She was, in turn, probably succeeded by Tutankhaten (later, Tutankhamun), with the country being administered by the chief vizier, and future Pharaoh, Ay. Tutankhamun is believed by some to be a younger brother of Smenkhkare and a son of Akhenaten, and possibly Kiya although one scholar has suggested that Tutankhamun may have been a son of Smenkhkare instead.

It has been suggested that after the death of Akhenaten, Nefertiti reigned with the name of Neferneferuaten but other scholars believe this female ruler was rather Meritaten. The so-called Coregency Stela, found in a tomb in Amarna possibly shows his queen Nefertiti as his coregent, ruling alongside him, but this is not certain as the names have been removed and recarved to show Ankhesenpaaten and Neferneferuaten.

With Akhenaten's death, the Aten cult he had founded gradually fell out of favour. Tutankhaten changed his name

to Tutankhamun in Year 2 of his reign (1332 BC) and abandoned the city of Akhetaten, which eventually fell into ruin. His successors Ay and Horemheb disassembled temples Akhenaten had built, including the temple at Thebes, using them as a source of easily available building materials and decorations for their own temples.

Present day Akhetaten

Finally, Akhenaten, Neferneferuaten, Smenkhkare, Tutankhamun, and Ay were excised from the official lists of Pharaohs, which instead reported that Amenhotep III was immediately succeeded by Horemheb. This is thought to be part of an attempt by Horemheb to delete all trace of Atenism and the pharaohs associated with it from the historical record. Akhenaten's name never appeared on any of the king lists compiled by later Pharaohs and it was not until the late 19th century that his identity was re-discovered and the surviving traces of his reign were unearthed by archaeologists.

As has been previously stated, in the early years of his reign, Amenhotep IV lived at Thebes with Nefertiti and his 6 daughters. Initially, he permitted worship of Egypt's traditional deities to continue but near the Temple of Karnak (Amun-Ra's great cult center), he erected several massive buildings including temples to the Aten, who was usually depicted as a sun disc.

These buildings at Thebes were later dismantled by his successors and used as infill for new constructions in the Temple of Karnak; when they were later dismantled by archaeologists, some 36,000 decorated blocks from the original Aten building here were revealed which preserve many elements of the original relief scenes and inscriptions. In honor of Aten, Akhenaten had over sawn the construction of some of the most massive temple complexes in ancient Egypt.

Bust of Horemheb

In these new temples, Aten was worshipped in the open sunlight, rather than in dark temple enclosures, as had been the previous custom. Akhenaten is also believed to have composed the Great Hymn to the Aten.

Initially, Akhenaten presented Aten as a variant of the familiar supreme deity Amun-Re (itself the result of an earlier rise to prominence of the cult of Amun, resulting in Amun becoming merged with the sun god Ra), in an attempt to put his ideas in a familiar Egyptian religious context. However, by Year 9 of his reign, he declared that Aten was not merely the supreme god, but the only god, and that he, Akhenaten, was the only intermediary between Aten and his people. He ordered the defacing of Amun's temples throughout Egypt and, in a number of instances, inscriptions of the plural 'gods' were also removed.

Aten's name is also written differently after Year 9, to emphasize the radicalism of the new regime, which included a ban on images, with the exception of a rayed solar disc, in which the rays (commonly depicted ending in hands) appear to represent the unseen spirit of Aten, who by then was evidently considered not merely a sun god, but rather a universal deity. Representations of the Aten were always accompanied with a sort of "hieroglyphic footnote", stating that the representation of the sun as all-encompassing Creator was to be taken as just that; a representation of something that, by its very nature as something transcending creation, cannot be fully or adequately represented by any one part of that creation.

Akhenaten's status as a religious revolutionary has led to much speculation, ranging from bona fide scholarly hypotheses to the non-academic fringe theories. Although many believe that he introduced or reintroduced monotheism, others see Akhenaten as a practitioner of an Aten monolatry, as he did not actively deny the existence of other gods; he simply refrained from worshipping any but the Aten while expecting the people to worship not Aten but him.

The idea of Akhenaten as the pioneer of a monotheistic religion that later became Judaism has been considered by various scholars. One of the first to mention this was Sigmund Freud, the founder of psychoanalysis, in his book *Moses and Monotheism*.

Sigmund Freud

Freud argued that Moses had been an Atenist priest forced to leave Egypt with his followers after Akhenaten's death and also argued that Akhenaten was striving to promote monotheism, something that the biblical Moses was able to achieve. Following his book, the concept entered popular consciousness and serious research. Other scholars and mainstream Egyptologists point out that there are direct connections between early Judaism and other Semitic religious traditions. They also state that two of the three principal Judaic terms for God, Yahweh, Elohim (morphologically plural, lit. "gods"), and Adonai (lit. "my lord") have a connection to Aten. Freud commented on the connection between Adonai, the Egyptian Aten and the Syrian divine name of Adonis as a primeval unity of language between the factions; in this he was following the argument of Egyptologist Arthur Weigall.

ADONAI

יְנִדָּא

LORD, MASTER
- Psalm 16:2 -

Jan Assmann's opinion is that 'Aten' and 'Adonai' are not linguistically related. Although there are similarities between Akhenaten's monotheistic experiment and the biblical story of Moses that have been explored in mainstream culture they include the idea that Akhenaten is the real character for the mythical Moses and Amarna the place as a literary misinterpretation of God raining an unknown fruit called manna while the Jews were wandering in the desert and the concept of a deity directing a group to a promised place which is the main theme in both stories.

Ahmed Osman has claimed that Akhenaten's maternal grandfather Yuya was the same person as the Biblical Joseph. Yuya held the title "Overseer of the Cattle of Min at Akhmin" during his life.

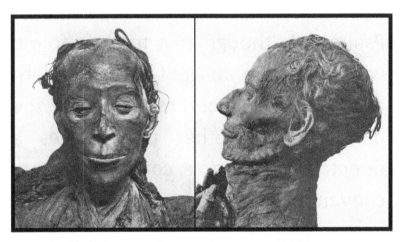

Akhenaten's grandparents Tuya and Yuya

He likely belonged to the local nobility of Akhmim. Egyptologists hold this view because Yuya had strong connections to the city of Akhmim in Upper Egypt. This makes it unlikely that he was a foreigner since most Asiatic settlers tended to cloister around the Nile Delta region of Lower Egypt. Some Egyptologists, however, give him a Mitannian origin. It is widely accepted that there are strong similarities between Akhenaten's Great Hymn to the Aten and the Biblical Psalm 104, though this form is found widespread in ancient Near Eastern hymnology both before and after the period and whether this implies a direct influence or a common literary convention remains in dispute.

Others have likened some aspects of Akhenaten's relationship with the Aten to the relationship, in Christian tradition, of Jesus Christ with God, particularly in interpretations that emphasize a more monotheistic interpretation of Atenism than henotheistic. Donald B. Redford has noted that some have viewed Akhenaten as a harbinger of Jesus. "After all, Akhenaten did call himself the son of the sole god: 'Thine only son that came forth from thy body'." James Henry Breasted likened him to Jesus, Arthur Weigall saw him as a failed precursor of Christ and Thomas Mann saw him "as right on the way and yet not the right one for the way".

Redford argued that while Akhenaten called himself the son of the Sun Disc and acted as the chief mediator between god and creation, kings for thousands of years before Akhenaten's time had claimed the same relationship and priestly role. However Akhenaten's case may be different through the emphasis placed on the heavenly father and son relationship. Akhenaten described himself as "thy son who came forth from thy limbs", "thy child", "the eternal son that came forth from the Sun Disc", and "thine only son that came forth from thy body". The close relationship between father and son is such that only the king truly knows the heart of "his father", and in return his father listens to his son's prayers. He is his father's image on earth and as Akhenaten is king on earth his father is king in heaven. As high priest, prophet, king and divine he claimed the central position in the new religious system. Since only he knew his father's mind and will, Akhenaten alone could interpret that will for all mankind with true teaching coming only from him.

Redford concluded:

'Before much of the archaeological evidence from Thebes and from Tell el-Amarna became available, wishful thinking sometimes turned Akhenaten into a humane teacher of the true God, a mentor of Moses, a Christ like figure, a philosopher before his time. But these imaginary creatures are now fading away one by one as the historical reality gradually emerges. There is little or no evidence to support the notion that Akhenaten was a progenitor of the full blown monotheism that we find in the Bible. The monotheism of the Hebrew Bible and the New Testament had its own separate development, one that began more than half a millennium after the pharaoh's death.'

Akhenaten portrayed in the Amarna style

However, Greenberg argues that Judaism shows signs that in its early forms it had Henotheistic characteristics and that it later was refined into a monotheism around the time of King Josiah, relegating that which previously were considered gods, into gods that ought not be worshipped, i.e. angels.

The rather strange and eccentric portrayals of Akhenaten, with a sagging stomach, thick thighs, large breasts, and long, thin face, so different from the athletic norm in the portrayal of Pharaohs, have led certain Egyptologists to suppose that Akhenaten suffered some kind of genetic abnormality. Various illnesses have been put forward. On the basis of his long jaw and his feminine appearance, Cyril Aldred, following up earlier arguments of Grafton Elliot Smith and James Strachey, suggested he may have suffered from Froelich's Syndrome, also known as Adiposogenital Dystrophy, which is a rare acquired disorder that occurs, either due to a tumorous growth near the pituitary gland in the brain, or due to a dysfunctional hypothalamus (an organ lying close to the pituitary.)

However, this is unlikely because this disorder results in sterility and Akhenaten is known to have fathered numerous children, who are repeatedly portrayed through years of archaeological and iconographic evidence.

Another suggestion by Burridge is that Akhenaten may have suffered from

Marfan's Syndrome, which, unlike Froelich's, does not result in any lack of intelligence or sterility. It is associated with a sunken chest, long curved spider-like fingers (arachnodactyly), occasional congenital heart difficulties, a high curved or slightly cleft palate, and a highly curved cornea or dislocated lens of the eye, with the requirement for bright light to see well. Marfan's sufferers tend towards being taller than average, with a long, thin face, and elongated skull, overgrown ribs, a funnel or pigeon chest, and larger pelvis, with enlarged thighs and spindly calves. Marfan's syndrome is a dominant characteristic, and sufferers have a 50% chance of passing it on to their children. All of these symptoms arguably sometimes appear in depictions of Akhenaten and of his children.

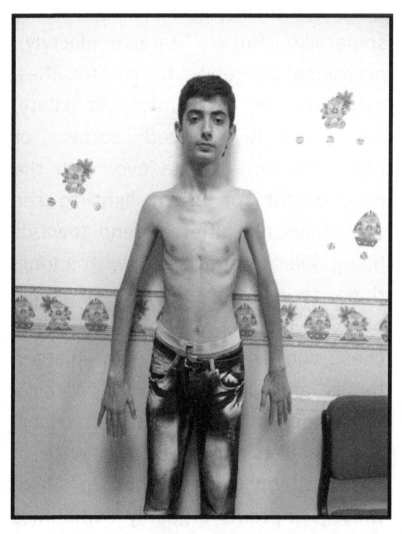

Modern child with Marfan's syndrome

Recent CT scans of Tutankhamun report a cleft palate and a fairly long head, as well as an abnormal curvature of the spine and fusion of the upper vertebrae, a condition associated with scoliosis, which are all conditions associated with Marfan's syndrome.

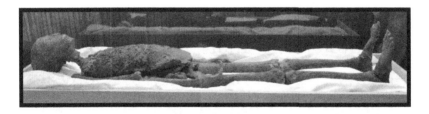

Body of Tutankhamun

However, DNA tests on Tutankhamun, in 2010, proved negative for Marfan syndrome. More recently, Homocystinuria was suggested as a possible diagnosis. Patients suffering from homocystinuria have Marfan symptoms, however, as an autosomal recessive disease it seems to fit better into Akhenaten's family tree. It is believed that Akhenaten's parents, Amenhotep III and Tiye, were most probably healthy.

However, Dominic Montserrat in *Akhenaten: History, Fantasy and Ancient Egypt* states that "there is now a broad consensus among Egyptologists that the exaggerated forms of Akhenaten's physical portrayal are not to be read literally". Montserrat and others argue that the body shape relates to some form of religious symbolism. Because the god Aten was referred to as "the mother and father of all humankind" it has been suggested that Akhenaten was made to perhaps look androgynous in artwork as a symbol of the androgyny of the god. This required "a symbolic gathering of all the attributes of the creator god into the physical body of the king himself", which will "display on earth the Aten's multiple life-giving functions".

Akhenaten did refer to himself as "The Unique One of Re", and he may have used his control of artistic expression to distance himself from the common people, though such a radical departure from the idealized traditional representation of the image of the Pharaoh would be truly extraordinary.

Another claim was made by Immanuel Velikovsky, who hypothesized an incestuous relationship with his mother, Tiye. Velikovsky also posited that Akhenaten had swollen legs.

Based on this, he identified Akhenaten as the history behind the Oedipus myth, Oedipus being Greek for "swollen feet", and moved the setting from the Greek Thebes to the Egyptian Thebes. As part of his argument, Velikovsky uses the fact that Akhenaten viciously carried out a campaign to erase the name of his father, which he argues could have developed into Oedipus killing his father. This point was disproved, in that Akhenaten mummified and buried his father in the honorable traditional Egyptian fashion prior to beginning his monotheistic revolution. Furthermore, an autopsy and genetic evidence in 2014 seemingly showed that Tutankhamun was the product of a brother-sister marriage, not a parent-child pairing.

Recently a surgeon at Imperial College London (Hutan Ashrafian) has analysed the early death of Akhenaten and the premature deaths of other Eighteenth dynasty Pharaohs (including Tutankhamun and Thutmose IV).

Likely Akhenaten and Nefertiti

He identifies that their early deaths were likely a result of a Familial Temporal Epilepsy. This would account for the untimely death of Akhenaten, his abnormal endocrine body shape on sculptures and can also explain Akhenaten's religious conviction due to this type of epilepsy's association with intense spiritual visions and religiosity.

It is the belief of authors such as Stephen Mehler, who wrote the brilliant *From Light Into Darkness; The Evolution Of Religion in Ancient Egypt,* that the reason why the mummies of Akhenaten, Nefertiti and the six daughters have never been positively identified could be because they were murdered, possibly at the same time, by the Amun priesthood. Moving his capital city to Amarna from Thebes and reducing, or possibly even eliminating their influence not only over the royal family but also the general public would have greatly restricted their incomes, or even eliminating them.

A great hatred would have arisen among these priests, and quite possibly that could have laid plans for, and carried out the murder of the royal family. Tutankhamun, whether the son or nephew of Akhenaten, was spared, so as to not create a vacuum in the presence of at least a symbol of royalty being present. But 3 years after the fall of Akhetaten he was moved back to Thebes, and his name changed, likely forcefully, from Tutankhaten to Tutankhamun. He is believed by most accounts to have become Pharaoh at the age of 9 or 10, and died about 11 years later. There are no surviving records of Tutankhamun's final days.

Reconstruction of Tutankhamun's possible appearance

What caused his death has been the subject of considerable debate. Major studies have been conducted in an effort to establish the cause of death, and there is some evidence, advanced by Harvard University microbiologist Ralph Mitchell, that his burial may have been hurried. Mitchell reported that dark brown splotches on the decorated walls of Tutankhamun's burial chamber suggested that he had been entombed even before the paint had a chance to dry.

Although there is some speculation that Tutankhamun was assassinated, the consensus is that his death was accidental. A CT scan taken in 2005 showed that he had suffered a compound left leg fracture shortly before his death, and that the leg had become infected. DNA analysis conducted in 2010 showed the presence of malaria in his system, leading to the belief that malaria and Koehler disease combined led to his death. On 14 September 2012, ABC News presented a further theory about Tutankhamun's death, developed by Dr. Hutan Ashrafian, who believed that temporal lobe epilepsy caused a fatal fall which also broke Tutankhamun's leg.

In June 2010, German scientists said they believed there was evidence that he had died of sickle cell disease. Other experts, however, rejected the hypothesis of homozygous sickle cell disease based on survival beyond the age of 5 and the location of the osteonecrosis which is characteristic of Freiberg-Kohler syndrome rather than sickle-cell disease. Research conducted in 2005 by archaeologists, radiologists, and geneticists, who performed CT scans on the mummy found that he was not killed by a blow to the head, as previously thought. New CT images discovered congenital flaws, which are more common among the children of incest. Siblings are more likely to pass on twin copies of harmful genes, which is why children of incest more commonly manifest genetic defects.

As to the fate of Akhenaten, Nefertiti and the six daughters, Stephen Mehler and others contend that they were murdered and their bodies disfigured or even torn to pieces in order to ensure that they and their spirits could never move onward. Recent genetic testing has confirmed that the male mummy buried in KV 55 died in his fifties, ruling out the earlier proposition that the body was that of Smenkhare. It is thought by many that the mummy is in fact that of Akhenaten. Interestingly, it appears that this mummy was intentionally defiled by those with a religious or political motivation. His face mask was torn and his name obliterated, but precious objects were left in place, confirming that the damage was not the work of tomb robbers but persons with a religious or political motivation.

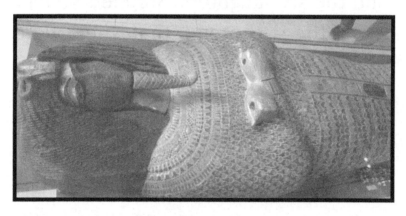

Coffin KV 55

There are many theories regarding the death and burial of Nefertiti, but to date, the mummy of this famous queen, her parents, or her children have not been found or formally identified. In 1898, archeologist Victor Loret found two female mummies inside the tomb of Amenhotep II in

KV35 in the Valley of the Kings. These two mummies, named 'The Elder Lady' and 'The Younger Lady', were likely candidates of her remains.

The KMT (a magazine on ancient Egypt published quarterly by Kmt communications) suggested in 2001 that the Elder Lady may be Nefertiti's body. It was argued that the evidence suggests that the mummy was around her mid-thirties or early forties, Nefertiti's guessed age of death.

Classic Nefertiti bust in the Neues Museum, Berlin, Germany

More evidence to support this identification was that the mummy's teeth look like that of a 29 to 38 year old, again Nefertiti's most likely age of death. Also, unfinished busts of Nefertiti appear to resemble the mummy's face, though other suggestions included Ankhesenamun.

Due to recent age tests on the mummy's teeth, it eventually became apparent that the 'Elder Lady' is in fact Queen Tiye, mother of Akhenaten and that the DNA of the mummy is a close, if not direct, match to the lock of hair found in Tutankhamun's tomb. The hair was found in a coffinette bearing an inscription naming Queen Tiye. Results have discovered that she was the daughter of Yuya and Thuya, who were the parents of Queen Tiye, thus ruling her out as Nefertiti.

On June 9, 2003, archaeologist Joann Fletcher, a specialist in ancient hair from the University of York in England, announced that Nefertiti's mummy may have been the Younger Lady. However, it is well known that an independent researcher, Marianne Luban, was the first person to suggest that the KV35 Young Lady could be Nefertiti in an online article, "Do We Have the Mummy of Nefertiti?" published in 1999. The team claimed that the mummy they examined was damaged in a way suggesting the body had been deliberately desecrated in antiquity. Mummification techniques, such as the use of embalming fluid and the presence of an intact brain, suggested an 18th dynasty royal mummy. Other elements which the team used to support their theory were the age of the body, the presence of embedded nefer beads, and a wig of a rare style worn by Nefertiti. They further claimed that the mummy's arm was originally bent in the position reserved for pharaohs, but was later snapped off and replaced with another arm in a normal position.

Most Egyptologists, among them Kent Weeks and Peter Lacovara, generally dismiss Fletcher's claims as unsubstantiated. They say that ancient mummies are almost impossible to identify as a particular person without DNA. As bodies of Nefertiti's parents or children have never been identified, her conclusive identification is impossible.

Any circumstantial evidence, such as hairstyle and arm position, is not reliable enough to pinpoint a single, specific historical person.

Profile of the famous Berlin bust of Nefertiti

9. Akhetaten: Amarna

Art typical of the Amarna period

The name Amarna comes from the Beni Amran tribe that lived in the region and founded a few settlements; prior to that of course it was called Akhetaten, which most translate as meaning "Horizon of the Aten." This could in fact have at least 2 meanings. As we have seen, Akhenaten distinguished himself in many ways, making him perhaps the most interesting of all of Egypt's pharaohs; he drastically changed the Egyptian belief system, heralded a new renaissance of art, including what some would consider exaggerated depictions of himself and his children, and moved the center of the Egyptian world from Thebes to Akhetaten.

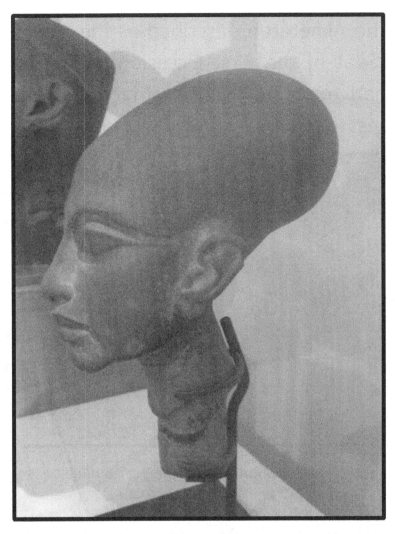

Stone bust of one of Akhenaten's daughters

The area of the city was effectively a virgin site, according to most academics, and it was in this city that the Akhetaten described as the Aten's "Seat of the First Occasion, which he had made for himself that he might rest in it."

Author Stephen Mehler paying homage to Akhenaten

Horizon of the Aten could refer to the fact that on the winter solstice the sun rises in a cleft between two mountains to the east. And another reference could very well be that Akhenaten built his capital on a far older site, quite possibly thousands of years older than the dynastic Egyptians. As he was clearly the keeper of profound ancient information, he likely knew that where he was to build his capital was truly very ancient.

The High Priest of Amun or First Prophet of Amun was the highest ranking priest in the priesthood of the Ancient Egyptian god Amun.

Members of the Khemit School exploring Akhetaten

The first high priests of Amun appear in the New Kingdom, at the beginning of the Eighteenth Dynasty. They gradually gained more and more power over the course of time, not simply spiritual but also economic, and a young Amenhotep IV would have witnessed this first hand at his father's court at Thebes.

During Amenhotep III's reign the worship of the Rising Sun, Harakhti, (not the metaphysical Re-Atum of the theologians but the red disk of the sun itself, Aten) gained many adherents at court. After the king's death, his widow Tiye became regent and brought up their son Amenhotep IV in an atmosphere inimical to the priesthood of Amen. The break with the Amun priests became even more serious when the construction of a great temple honoring Re-Harakhti was built right by the Amun temple at Karnak and when the pharaoh declared himself to be the First Prophet of Harakhti. From a letter found at Amarna addressed to Ramose, his vizier and director of prophets of the South and the North, even though he was not a priest of either Amen or

Aten, one can draw the conclusion that Amun's priests had reacted "unfavorably" to say the least. The pharaoh supposedly says:

'the actions of the priests are more perverted than those things I heard in year IV... more perverted than anything my father and my grandfather ever heard.'

By most accounts in year 6 of Amenhotep IV's reign the new city of Aten, Akhetaten, was founded and Amenhotep's name was changed to Akhenaten. All his family members took Aten-names as did the members of the court and the royal administration, and the government removed itself to Akhetaten (today's el Amarna). The abrupt cessation of funding had a devastating effect on the Amun temples:

'the land was as if during a time of chaos... the temples of the gods at Elephantine had fallen on ill times. The ruinous sanctuaries were abandoned... All the land was in distress. The gods averted their faces from this land...If you invoked the gods, they didn't heed the appeal.'

The Khemit School overlooking the site of Akhetaten

The fate of the priests is unknown but the wealth of the temples, their land and slaves, were probably confiscated by the crown, for unless economically ruined, the temples would not have been abandoned. To the followers of Amun this was a time of hardship and spiritual darkness caused by the god, yet they were certain that Amun would prevail, and that 'they', the worshipers of Aten, would lose their power. This hope was expressed in a graffito inscribed by Pawah, a scribe of the temple of Amun, on the door jamb of a Theban tomb:

'Turn your face towards us, O lord of eternity!

You were here before 'they' arose,

You will be here when 'they' are gone.

You caused me to see a darkness of your making.

Bestow light upon me, so that I may see you.'

Akhetaten, as has been previously stated was destroyed beyond recognition once Akhenaten was dead and Tutankhamun was back in Thebes. The city seems to have remained active for a decade or so after his death, and a shrine to Horemheb indicates that it was at least partially occupied at the beginning of his reign, if only as a source for building material elsewhere. Once it was abandoned it remained uninhabited until Roman settlement began along the edge of the Nile. However, due to the unique circumstances of its creation and abandonment, it is questionable how representative of ancient Egyptian cities it actually was.

In the spring of 2015 the author, along with the Khemit School based in Giza explored the ancient site of Akhetaten. The city itself had been completely recycled over time for its building stone, and the millions of mud bricks which had comprised the bulk of the city were now mere dust. Such was the hatred of Akhenaten by the Amun priesthood. However, large chambers, off limits much of the time, yet opened for us, revealed that Akhenaten had built his "new" city on an extremely ancient site.

One of the massive ancient chambers at Akhetaten

The chambers were cut out of solid limestone bedrock, and as the photos show are quite vast in scale. As well, there are staircases carved into the bedrock going down at least one level. In Akhenaten's time, bronze was the hardest metal available in any great quantity, with iron appearing several hundreds of years later. It is more likely that these chambers and stairs came from a much more ancient time, when a previous civilization with advanced technology, who also made the Giza pyramids and tunnel systems in that area, were present. If such was the case, then Akhenaten had his artisans adorn the pre-existing walls with depictions of life during the pharaoh's time, both in relief carving and bright paints.

Depiction of Akhenaten and Nefertiti in one of the ancient chambers

What many do not realize is that in the oral tradition of Egypt, Ra or Re was not the only name of the sun, but was in fact one of 5 phases, and here they are, according to Stephen Mehler and his teacher Abd'El Hakim Awyan:

Kheper: dawn

Ra: noon

Oon: early to mid afternoon

Aten: late afternoon to twilight

Amun (or Amen): night-darkness

The 5 phases of the sun also represent the 5 stages of a human life, from birth to death, and 5 greater cycles of time. It could very well be that as Akhenaten was an adept initiate of the mystery schools of Egypt, and thus had access to the true knowledge of the great antiquity of Egyptian culture, which much longer than the dynastic periods, and that could have made him a threat to the Amun priests.

According to Mehler, the 5 stages represent both stages of consciousness and epochs of human prehistory and history. Kheper, the Driller symbolized by the scarab beetle, represents the birth of consciousness, the dawn. Ra, The Stubborn symbolized by the ram, characterizes the adolescent or early stages of consciousness; the sun at high noon. Oon, The Wise symbolized by a man standing upright with a staff, stands for adult or mature consciousness; the sun in the early afternoon. Aten, The Wiser symbolized by an old man hunched over with his staff, is the stage of enlightenment or full flowering of consciousness; the sun at full apex heading towards twilight. And finally Amun, The Hidden, who originally had no image, is the end of the cycle where we experience the loss of full consciousness, where truth is obfuscated or hidden; the night when all is in darkness.

Again according to Mehler, and based on teachings from his mentor Abd'El Hakim Awyan, the cycle of Amun, The Hidden began around 4000 BC. That would mean that this cycle began prior to the rise of the dynastic Egyptians, which likely occurred around 3100 BC. Prior to that would have been what Mehler and Abd'El Hakim regarded as a period of a higher state of consciousness, that of Aten.

Again according to their understanding of the ancient Suf language, which was that of the dynastic Egyptians, Akhenaten's original title (name) of Amenhotep means "The Offering to the Hidden One" whereas his adopted title of Akhenaten translates as "The Shade or Shadow of the Wiser" with

Akh meaning "shade" or "shadow" and Aten being "the Wiser."

It would appear that Akhenaten had a clear distaste for the Amun priesthood who clearly wanted to keep all ancient and esoteric knowledge hidden, but for also for his early name Amenhotep IV. He clearly did not wanted to be known as "the offering to the hidden" and thus changed his name to reflect his own belief system, that of the more enlightened Aten period which preceded that of Amun. Mehler and others, including the author believe that monotheism was a concept that existed in ancient Egypt long before Akhenaten was born. As an example, Hakim mentioned to Mehler that the Aten is mentioned in reliefs of the Third Dynasty of the Old Kingdom period, some 1500 years before Akhenaten's time.

Abd'El Hakim Awyan and Stephen Mehler

Akhenaten was not worshipping the disk of the sun, which was the symbol of the Aten for him, but light, as the illumination and elimination of darkness that the sun provides, and the elimination of ignorance that the light of enlightenment brings. Thus, what he was trying to do was to breech the darkness and hiddenness of the age of Amun, to break the power and corruption of the priests of Amun, and try to return to the high consciousness and pure spirituality of the age of Aten.

The question arises as to where or from whom Akhenaten first received the teachings which would make him make such radical decisions such as changing his name and moving his capital to a new location. As we have seen, he clearly hated the stranglehold of power by the Amun priesthood who likely regarded him as simply a puppet ruler to be controlled, but it appears that his mother was very influential on him as he was growing up.

Tiye is known to have been Akhenaten's mother, and her name/title, according to Hakim means "She Is The One" which would clearly indicate a woman of great power and influence. Her origins remain somewhat obscure. Some academics believe that her mummy was identified as "The Elder Lady" found in the tomb of Amenhotep II (KV35) in 2010, and that her father, Yuya, was a non-royal, wealthy landowner from the Upper Egyptian town of Akhmin; a city in the Sohag Governorate. There he served as a priest and superintendent of oxen or commander of the chariotry. Tiye's mother, Thuya, was involved in many religious cults, as her different titles attested (Singer of Hathor, Chief of the Entertainers of both Amun and Min...), which suggests that she was a member of the royal family.

Egyptologists have suggested that Tiye's father, Yuya, was of foreign origin due to the features of his mummy and the many different spellings of his name, which might imply it was a non-Egyptian name in origin. It is possible that he came from the kingdom of Mitanni in what is now northern Syria. Some suggest that the queen's strong political and unconventional religious views might have been due not just to a strong character, but to foreign descent.

Tiye wielded a great deal of power during both her husband's and son's reigns. Amenhotep III became a fine sportsman, a lover of outdoor life, and a great statesman. He often had to

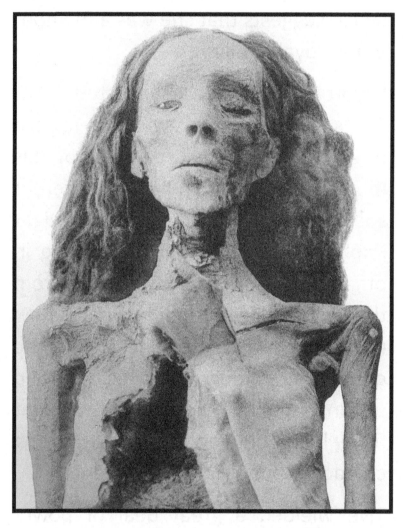

Mummy of Akhenaten's mother Tiye

consider claims for Egypt's gold and requests for his royal daughters in marriage from foreign kings such as Tushratta of Mitanni and Kadashman-Enlil I of Babylon. The royal lineage was carried by the women of Ancient Egypt and marriage to one would have been a path to the throne for their progeny. She became her husband's trusted adviser and confidant. Being wise, intelligent, strong, and fierce, she was able to gain the respect of foreign dignitaries. Foreign leaders were in fact willing to deal directly through her. She continued to play an active role in foreign relations and was the first Egyptian queen to have her name recorded on official acts.

Tiye may have continued to advise her son, Akhenaten, when he took the throne. Her son's correspondence with Tushratta, the king of Mitanni, speaks highly of the political influence she wielded at court. In Amarna letter EA 26, Tushratta, king of Mitanni, corresponded directly with Tiye to reminisce about the good relations he enjoyed with her then deceased husband and extended his wish to continue on friendly terms with her son, Akhenaten.

Unlike other pharaohs before his time, Akhenaten wanted to share the philosophy of Aten with not only the royal court, but the public at large. He commissioned many artworks during his time as pharaoh, paintings, wall engravings and sculptures, but most were destroyed by the Amun priests. He is portrayed, especially in the early part of his reign as we have seen, with an almost grotesque or even cartoon like appearance.

Akhenaten shown sacrificing a duck

From the photos of him in this book he is often shown with a long, hatchet like face, a swollen belly, feminine like hips and spindly legs. However, Stephen Mehler believes that this was an intentional exaggeration by the Aten priests who directed the sculptors and other artists to portray him that way. Akhenaten always used an appellation for himself, called Ankh-en-Ma'at, which has been translated as "living in truth." According to Mehler, the actual translation should be "living according to divine law." Mehler believes that Akhenaten used this expression to show that he was much more with living a true spiritual life and realizing the illusory and transitory nature of the physical world.

It is very possible that the Aten period artists went overboard as regards the portrayals of Akhenaten, including the fact that he had himself at times, and especially his daughters shown having elongated heads. According to Mehler, the most accurate of portrayals of

Akhenaten is a bust in the Berlin museum, in which he does look rather attractive and normal.

Busts of Akhenaten and Nefertiti in the Berlin Museum

The reason why he and his daughters were often depicted as having elongated heads could because he was not trying to describe what they actually looked like, but ancient ancestors who may have appeared to have had such features. As the time of Aten was prior to the accepted history of Egypt by most modern scholars, it could be that Akhenaten had access to secret knowledge of enlightened pre-dynastic people.

Two of the daughters carved in low relief

Scientific evidence is beginning to show, especially from geologists, that many of the famous ancient sites in Egypt are pre-dynastic, including the pyramids at Giza and Dashur, as well as the massive stone boxes in the Serapeum at Saqqara. Akhenaten may have been telling us, through the art that he descended from what most sources believe to have been a divine being, Osiris.

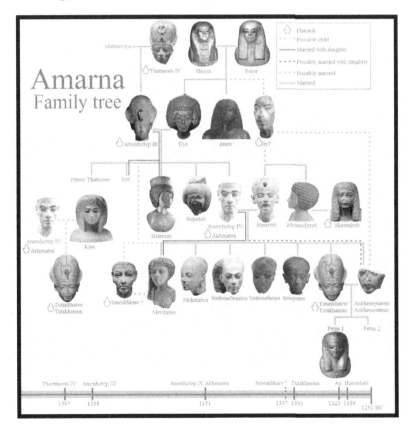

The Amarna family tree

Sculpture of Osiris

Osiris, alternatively Ausir, Asiri or Ausar, (among other spellings), usually identified as the god of the afterlife, the underworld, and the dead, but more appropriately as the god of transition, resurrection, and regeneration. He was classically depicted as a green-skinned man with a pharaoh's beard, partially mummy-wrapped at the legs, wearing a distinctive crown with two large ostrich feathers at either side, and holding a symbolic crook and flail. Osiris was at times considered the oldest son of the earth god Geb, though other sources state his father is the sun-god Ra and his mother the sky goddess Nut, as well as being brother and husband of Isis, with Horus being considered his posthumously begotten son. That is the conventional account.

Osiris is first attested in the middle of the Fifth dynasty of Egypt, although it is likely that he was worshipped much earlier; the Khenti-Amentiu epithet (an ancient Egyptian deity whose name was also used as a title for Osiris) dates to at least the first dynasty, also as a pharaonic title. Most information available on the myths of Osiris is derived from allusions contained in the Pyramid Texts at the end of the Fifth Dynasty, later New Kingdom source documents such as the Shabaka Stone (a relic from the Nubian Twenty-fifth Dynasty of Egypt incised with an Egyptian religious text) and the Contending of Horus and Seth, and much later, in narrative style from the writings of Greek authors including Plutarch and Diodorus Siculus.

Classic representation of Osiris

In Egyptian hieroglyphs the name is written Wsjr, as the hieroglyphic writing does not restitute all the vowels, and Egyptologists transliterate the name variously as Asar, Yasar, Aser, Asaru, Ausar, Ausir, Wesir, Usir, Usire or Ausare. Several proposals have been made for the etymology and meaning of the original name Wsjr. John Gwyn Griffiths (1980) proposed a derivation from wser signifying "the powerful". Moreover, one of the oldest attestations of the god Osiris appears in the mastaba of the deceased Netjer-wser (God Almighty).

However, Stephen Mehler and some others believe that the proper ancient name of Osiris is Wizzer, from which we get the English words wisdom and wizard, clearly describing someone of high knowledge. The most common myth story about Osiris is from Plutarch who recounts one version of the myth in which Set (Osiris' brother), along with the Queen of Ethiopia, conspired with 72 accomplices to plot the assassination of Osiris. Set fooled Osiris into getting into a box, which Set then shut, sealed with lead, and threw into the Nile. Osiris' wife, Isis, searched for his remains until she finally found him embedded in a tamarisk tree trunk, which was holding up the roof of a palace in Byblos on the Phoenician coast. She managed to remove the coffin and open it, but Osiris was already dead.

She used a spell learned from her father and brought him back to life so he could impregnate her. Afterwards he died again and she hid his body in the desert. Months later, she gave birth to Horus. While she raised Horus, Set was hunting one night and came across the body of Osiris. Enraged, he tore the body into fourteen pieces and scattered them throughout the land. Isis gathered up all the parts of the body, except the penis (which had been eaten by a fish, the medjed) and bandaged them together for a proper burial.

Of course, it is believed by most that Osiris, Isis and Horus are and were fictitious characters. No trace of their skeletons have ever been found, yet there are many references which state that Osiris was once a living ruler that travelled the world teaching civilization. This would have clearly been during the time known as pre-dynastic, and such an idea is shunned by the majority of academics.

The author believes that least visually, in terms of allowing his artists to portray his daughters, and perhaps himself with an elongated head, that he was referring to his descent from an either earthly, or divine Osiris. But above all, it was his love and adherence to the Aten that ruled supreme.

10. Conclusions

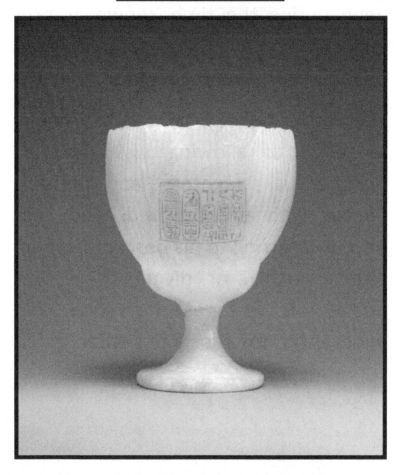

Cup of Amenhotep IV and Nefertiti

Akhenaten was a "God-intoxicated man," whose mind responded with marvelous sensitiveness and discernment to the visible evidences of the Aten about him. He was absolutely ecstatic in his sense of the beauty of the eternal and universal light. In this respect Akhenaten's revolution consisted of the gospel of beauty and beneficence of the natural order, a recognition of the message of nature to the soul of man. The breath of nature had touched life and art at the same time and quickened them with a new vision. Even the pharaoh's relations with his family became natural and unrestrained. Like all true revolutions it affected all aspects of man's life. He was determined to establish a world of things as they are, in wholesome naturalness. Such fundamental changes as these, on a moment's reflection, suggest what an overwhelming tide of inherited thought, custom, and tradition had been diverted from its channel by the young ruler who was guiding this revolution.

It is only as this aspect of his movement is clearly discerned that we begin to appreciate the power of his remarkable personality. Before his time religious documents were usually attributed to ancient rulers and wise men, and the power of a belief lay chiefly in its claim to remote antiquity and the sanctity of immemorial custom. Until Akhenaten the history of the world had been but the irresistible drift of tradition. All men had been but drops of water in the great current. Akhenaten was possibly the first individual in history. Consciously and deliberately, by intellectual process he gained his position, and then placed himself squarely in the face of tradition and swept it aside.

Damaged figures, likely of Nefertiti and Akhenaten at Akhetaten

What did this revolution mean to the Egyptian people? How did it affect their daily life? The whole environment of existence changed. Their holy places had been desecrated, the shrines sacred with the memories of thousands of years had been closed up, the priests driven away, the offerings and temple incomes confiscated, and the old order blotted out. Groups of muttering priests, nursing implacable hatred, must have mingled their curses with the execration of whole communities of discontented tradesmen; those who had made a comfortable living out of the old religion. Bakers no longer made a living from the sale of ceremonial cakes at the temple feasts. Craftsmen no longer sold holy trinkets of the old gods at the temple gateway. Tombstone makers and scribes who had sold their cheap wares to a gullible public were bankrupt.

Actors and priestly mimes were driven away from the sacred groves of Osiris by the police. Normally they would have presented the passion play, reenacting the drama of the life, death and resurrection of Osiris. Physicians no longer collected money for expelling evil spirits. Shepherds no longer placed a loaf of bread and jar of water under a tree in order to placate the goddess of the tree who might otherwise bring sickness to the household. Peasants no longer erected crude images of the gods in the field to drive away terrible demons of drought and famine.

Amarna stelae 3 at Akhetaten

Mothers no longer dared to pray with their little ones at bedtime to shield them from the demons of darkness. In the midst of a whole land thus darkened by clouds of smoldering discontent, this marvelous young pharaoh, and the group of sympathizers who served under him set up their tabernacle to the daily light, in serene unconsciousness of the total darkness that enveloped all around and grew daily darker and more threatening.

When we place the revolutionary movement of Akhenaten against this background of popular discontent and then add to it the secret opposition of a powerful priesthood, a powerful army which disliked his peace policy, we begin to appreciate the powerful individuality of this intellectual leader in history. His reign was the earliest age of the rule of ideas. Akhenaten was possibly the world's first revolutionary, and he was fully convinced that he might entirely recast the world of religion, thought, and life by the invincible purpose he held. Like all true revolutionaries at all times Akhenaten was seemingly fully persuaded that his ideas were right and that all would eventually benefit by them.

These are believed to have been some of Akhenaten's quotes:

"True wisdom is less presuming than folly. The wise man doubteth often, and changeth his mind; the fool is obstinate, and doubteth not; he knoweth all things but his own ignorance."

"Honor is the inner garment of the Soul; the first thing put on by it with the flesh, and the last it layeth down at its separation from it."

"Be thou incapable of change in that which is right, and men will rely upon thee. Establish unto thyself principles of action; and see that thou ever act according to them. First know that thy principles are just, and then be thou."

"Say not that honor is the child of boldness, nor believe thou that the hazard of life alone can pay the price of it; it is not to the action that it is due, but to the manner of performing it."

"Labor not after riches first, and think thou afterwards wilt enjoy them. He who neglecteth the present moment, throweth away all that he hath. As the arrow passeth through the heart, while the warrior knew not that it was."

"Indulge not thyself in the passion of anger; it is whetting a sword to wound thine own breast, or murder thy friend."

"The ambitious will always be first in the crowd; he presseth forward, he looketh not behind him. More anguish is it to his mind to see one before him, than joy to leave thousands at a distance."

"As the ostrich when pursued hideth his head, but forgetteth his body; so the fears of a coward expose him to danger."

"As a rock on the seashore he standeth firm, and the dashing of the waves disturbeth him not. He raiseth his head like a tower on a hill, and the arrows of fortune drop at his feet. In the instant of danger, the courage of his heart here, and scorn to fly."

"As the whirlwind in its fury teareth up trees, and deformeth the face of nature, or as an earthquake in its convulsions overturneth whole cities; so the rage of an angry man throweth mischief around him."

Made in the USA
Las Vegas, NV
14 February 2024

85776533R00085